Georgia, My State
Rocks and Minerals

Rocks and Minerals
of the
Coastal Plain

by Samantha Stanford

STATE STANDARDS PUBLISHING®

Your State • Your Standards • Your Grade Level

Dear Educators, Librarians and Parents . . .

Thank you for choosing the *"Georgia, My State"* Series! We have designed this series to support the Georgia Department of Education's Georgia Performance Standards for elementary level Georgia studies. Each book in the series has been written at appropriate grade level as measured by the ATOS Readability Formula for Books (Accelerated Reader), the Lexile Framework for Reading, and the Fountas & Pinnell Benchmark Assessment System for Guided Reading. Photographs and/or illustrations, captions, and other design elements have been included to provide supportive visual messaging to enhance text comprehension. Glossary and Word Index sections introduce key new words and help young readers develop skills in locating and combining information.

We wish you all success in using the *"Georgia, My State"* Series to meet your student or child's learning needs. For additional sources of information, see www.georgiaencyclopedia.org.

Jill Ward, President

Publisher
State Standards Publishing, LLC
1788 Quail Hollow
Hamilton, GA 31811
USA
1.866.740.3056
www.statestandardspublishing.com

Library of Congress Control Number: 2010933589

Printed in the United States of America, North Mankato, Minnesota, August 2010, 082010.

About the Author

Samantha Stanford graduated with honors from Columbus State University in Columbus, Georgia with a degree in geology. She is pursuing a Master of Science in geology at the University of North Carolina at Wilmington, with plans to earn a doctorate in paleontology. Her research has been published in the *New Mexico Museum of Natural History & Science Bulletins* and featured in *National Geographic Daily News*. She enjoys spending her free time collecting fossils with her husband, Chris, and their dogs, Maya and Caiman.

Table of Contents

The Rock Cycle

Cools and Lifts

Igneous Rock

Magma

Erosion

Melting

Sediment

Metamorphic Rock

Heat and Pressure Underground

Pressed Together Under Water

Sedimentary Rock

4

What are Rocks and Minerals?

Hi, I'm Bagster. Let's explore rocks and minerals in Georgia! A **mineral** is a natural material that is not alive like plants and animals. A **rock** is made of two or more minerals. Think of a rock as being like a cake. The flour, butter, and eggs in the cake would be minerals. The whole cake would be the rock. There are three kinds of rocks. **Igneous** rocks are made from hot liquid rock called **magma**. **Sedimentary** rocks are made from igneous rocks. Rain and wind break the rocks into tiny pieces called **sediment**. This process is called **erosion**. **Metamorphic** rocks form when igneous or sedimentary rocks are pushed underground and heat up. Rocks can change from one type to another and back again. This process is called the **rock cycle**.

Most of the soil is soft and sandy.

Appalachian Plateau

Blue Ridge Mountains

Valley and Ridge

Piedmont

Fall Line

Coastal Plain

The Coastal Plain had a sea and beaches long ago!

Sandy Coastal Plain

Let's explore the Coastal Plain **geographic region**. A region is an area named for the way the land is formed. The Coastal Plain sits below the Piedmont region. It is separated by the **fall line**. The fall line is a strip of land that falls steeply.

The Coastal Plain is Georgia's largest geographic region. It has lots of minerals that come from hard rocks in the Piedmont region. There is a lot of sand here. Most of the ground is soft and sandy. Do you know why? The Coastal Plain looked much different millions of years ago. It was once a coast! The Coastal Plain was covered in water. It had a sea and beaches long ago!

Hard rock breaks into smaller pieces.

Minerals come back to the beach.

Sand

River

Minerals   Minerals

Minerals wash into streams and rivers.

Ocean

Minerals from River

Minerals wash out to the ocean.

8

Why So Sandy?

Have you ever wondered why there's sand at the beach? Hard rock erodes over time. It breaks into smaller pieces. The minerals fall out. The minerals and small pieces of rock wash into streams and rivers. They tumble around in the water. They lose their sharp edges. Next, streams and rivers wash the minerals out to the ocean. Ocean waves bring the minerals back to the beach. The minerals pile up and make sand.

Sand is made of billions of tiny pieces of quartz and other minerals. All of these pieces came from hard rock above the coast. When you go to the beach, imagine where the sand came from. It could have traveled hundreds of miles!

Sand is made of quartz and other minerals.

Glass Making

Drink Coaster

Sandstone can be carved into different shapes, like statues.

Superb Sandstone

The Coastal Plain has more than just sand. There is also a lot of sandstone here. Sandstone is a sedimentary rock made of sand that has been **compacted**, or pressed together. It's easy to remember sandstone because it's made from sand!

Sandstone is soft. It crumbles easily. It's not strong enough to use for building heavy things. Sandstone is used in making glass. Drink coasters are sometimes made of sandstone. They help catch the water that drips down the glass. Sandstone can be carved into different shapes, like statues and fountains. Crumbled sandstone is also used in making roadways. The roads you travel could have minerals in them that came from the Coastal Plain!

Sandstone

Household Cleaner

Sink, Toilet, and Tub

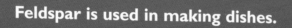

Feldspar is used in making dishes.

Fancy Feldspar

Feldspar is the most common mineral on the entire earth! Feldspar is found in igneous rocks like granite. It's found in sedimentary rocks like sandstone. It's also found in metamorphic rocks like gneiss. Many beach sands have tiny grains of feldspar in them. Feldspar is usually a light pink color. You can tell feldspar apart from other minerals because it has tiny white lines in it. These are called **striations**.

Feldspar is used in household cleaners that scrub things. It's used in making sinks, toilets, and tubs. It's also used to make dishes. People use feldspar every day!

Striations

Feldspar is the most common mineral on the entire earth!

Jewelry

Hematite turns things red, like rust.

Hematite makes soil in Providence Canyon red.

Hooray for Hematite!

Hematite is found in sedimentary rocks and metamorphic rocks of the Coastal Plain. It comes in different colors and shapes. Sometimes hematite is shiny and silver. Sometimes it's red and lumpy. How can you tell if a mineral is hematite? By its streak! Hematite has iron in it. Iron is a **metal** that rusts. It turns things red. Metal is a substance that conducts heat or electricity. Hematite leaves a red streak when you rub it against a smooth surface. Hematite sometimes makes soil in the Coastal Plain red.

Hematite is used to make jewelry. It is also used to dye things red and brown. You can find lots of hematite in Providence Canyon near Lumpkin!

Hematite comes in different colors and shapes.

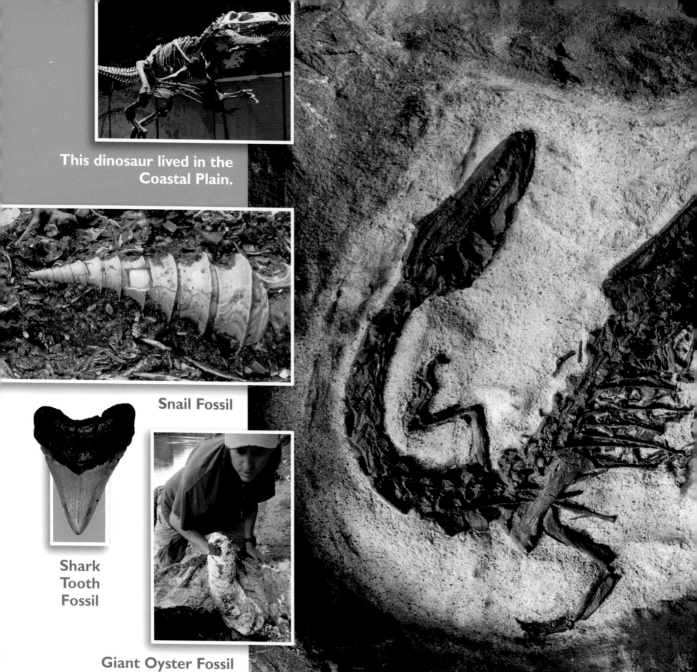

This dinosaur lived in the Coastal Plain.

Snail Fossil

Shark Tooth Fossil

Giant Oyster Fossil

Animal bones and shells can become fossils.

Finding Fossils

It's easy to find **fossils** in the Coastal Plain. Fossils are the remains of plants or animals that lived long ago. Like dinosaurs! When an animal dies, it leaves its bones or shell behind. The bones sometimes get buried by soil and water. Sometimes the bones turn into rocks and minerals. This is how fossils are formed.

Paleontologists have found all kinds of fossils in the Coastal Plain. Paleontologists are scientists who study fossils. They've found fossils of turtles and snails. They've found dinosaur fossils. They've even found fossils of sharks and giant oysters here!

Toothpaste

Lightbulb

People mine kaolin in Georgia.

An Everyday Mineral

Have you ever poured milk from a plastic bottle or drawn on a piece of paper? Have you ever kicked a rubber kickball? Plastic, paper, and rubber are all made from a mineral called kaolin. Kaolin is found where the Piedmont meets the Coastal Plain region. It's not hard like most minerals. It's a type of clay. Kaolin is very smooth. It's white and looks like the chalk teachers use. It even feels the same as chalk. Lots of things have kaolin in them, like toothpaste. Even light bulbs have kaolin in them.

Georgia has lots of kaolin near Sandersville. People **mine** kaolin here. They dig it out of the ground. Kaolin is very valuable to our state!

Kaolin

Aluminum Foil

Aluminum Roof

Aluminum Cans

Cars are made of aluminum from bauxite.

Banking on Bauxite

Do you drink soda? An important rock from the Coastal Plain helps make the soda cans you drink from. This rock is called bauxite. People mine bauxite near Andersonville. Bauxite is an **ore**. An ore is a rock that contains metal. The metal in bauxite is called aluminum. Bauxite looks something like the inside of a peanut candy bar! It has large grains that sit inside a smooth body.

We get aluminum from bauxite. We wrap things in aluminum foil to cook them. We put aluminum on the roofs of houses. We eat food from aluminum cans. Cars and trucks are made with aluminum from bauxite. Bauxite is a very useful rock!

Bauxite

Glossary

compacted – Pressed together.

erosion – The process of breaking rock into sediment.

fall line – A strip of land that falls steeply.

fossils – The remains of plants or animals that lived long ago.

geographic region – An area named for the way the land is formed.

igneous – Rocks that are made from magma.

magma – Hot liquid rock.

metal – A substance that conducts heat or electricity.

metamorphic – Rocks made when igneous or sedimentary rocks are pushed underground and heat up.

mine – To dig up a rock or a mineral from underground.

mineral – A natural material that is not alive like plants and animals.

ore – A rock that contains metal.

paleontologists – Scientists who study fossils.

rock – A material that is made of two or more minerals.

rock cycle – The process by which rocks change from one type to another.

sediment – Tiny pieces of rocks broken up by rain and wind.

sedimentary – Rocks that are made from igneous rocks.

striations – Tiny lines found in minerals like feldspar.

Word Index

Image Credits

p. 4   Igneous rock: © River North Photography, iStockphotography.com; Sediment: © iEverest, iStockphotography.com; Sedimentary rock: © Stephen Morris, iStockphotography.com; Metamorphic rock: © Gene Krebs, iStockphotography.com; Magma: © Thuerig Manfred, iStockphotography.com

p. 6   Dinosaur: © Linda Bucklin, iStockphotography.com; Child's foot: © Sweety Mommy, iStockphotography.com

p. 8   Rock: © Roberto Gennaro, iStockphotography.com; River: © Paulo Ferreria, iStockphotography.com; Ocean: Photo courtesy of Gray's Reef National Marine Sanctuary; Beach: © Dawn Nichols, iStockphotography.com; Sand: © Alexandr Malyshev, iStockphotography.com

p. 9   Quartz: © Francisco Romero, iStockphotography.com

p. 10   Statues: © Simon Podgorsek, iStockphotography.com; Glass making: © Syagci, iStockphotography.com; Drink coaster: © Jesse Kunerth, iStockphotography.com; Beverage: © Sidsnapper, iStockphotography.com

p. 11   Sandstone sample: © Don Nichols, iStockphotography.com

p. 12   Dishes: © Megapixel Media, iStockphotography.com; Sponge: © Stephan Zabel, iStockphotography.com; Bathroom: © Peter Mukjerhee, iStockphotography.com

p. 13   Feldspar sample: © Tyler Boyes, fotolia.com

p. 14   Providence Canyon: Photo courtesy of Georgia Department of Economic Development; Jewelry: © Christine Lamour, fotolia.com; Screw: © Arne Thaysen, iStockphotography.com

p.15   Silver hematite: © Chris Crowley, iStockphotography.com; Red hematite: © Remi Bonet, fotolia.com; Hematite streak: © Wek Wek, iStockphotography.com

p. 16   Animal fossil: © Michael Gray, iStockphotography.com; Dinosaur skeleton (Appalachiosaurus), snail fossil, oyster fossil: © Alan Cressler, Flickr.com; Shark tooth fossil: © Mark Kostich, iStockphotography.com

p. 17   Dinosaur: © Linda Bucklin, iStockphotography.com

p. 18   Kaolin mine: Photo courtesy of Georgia Department of Economic Development; Tooth brushing: © Andreas Gradin, iStockphotography.com; Light bulb: © Denis Vorob\'yev, iStockphotography.com; Kaolin sample: Photo courtesy of United States Geological Survey, © Earth Science World Image Bank

p. 20   Automobile: © Smirnov Vasily, iStockphotography.com; Foil: © Lauri Patterson, iStockphotography.com; Roof: © Dick Stada, iStockphotography.com; Cans: © Todd Taulman, iStockphotography.com

p. 21   Bauxite sample: © FokinOl, iStockphotography.com

Editorial Credit

Designer: Michael Sellner, Corporate Graphics, North Mankato, Minnesota

Georgia, My State Rocks and Minerals

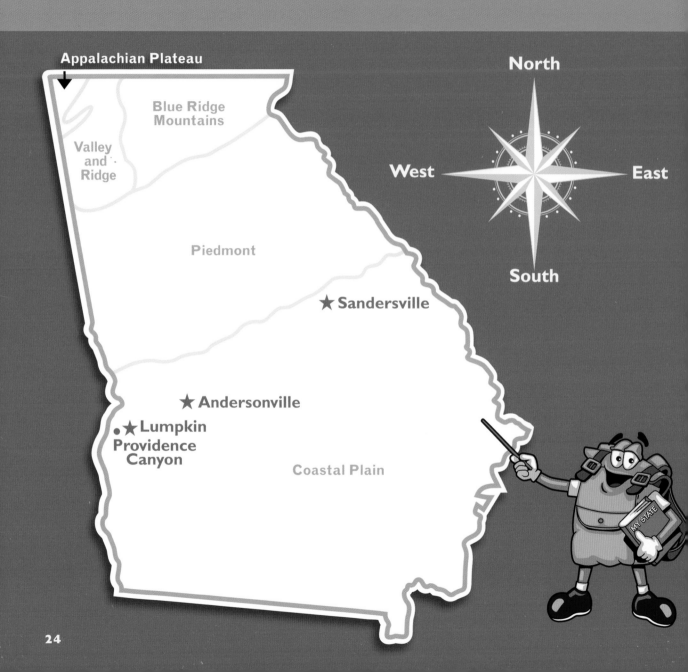

Appalachian Plateau

Blue Ridge Mountains

Valley and Ridge

Piedmont

★ Sandersville

★ Andersonville

●★ Lumpkin
Providence Canyon

Coastal Plain

North

West

East

South

MY STATE